Making Needle-Felting Magic

New Techniques, Creative Projects

MARGO DUKE

Martingale®
& COMPANY

Dedication

To those who adore fiber and flowers, bountiful treasures, and blessings of the earth. These gifts from God are readily available and together with my needle-felting machine have provided me with endless delight and pleasure; for that I am truly thankful. I've found my Bliss.

Acknowledgments

Special thanks are due to my husband, Peter, for keeping my body and spirit nourished through endless hours spent in my studio and during all the phases of these projects: concept, design, experimentation, and implementation.

I'd also like to express my gratitude to those folks at Martingale & Company who had the foresight to support my notion of a growing demand for more machine needle-felting projects. Further thanks to Nancy Mahoney, my technical editor, who had the responsibility of plowing through the myriad of details to help it all make sense, and to Sheila Ryan, my copy editor, for her expertise.

Making More Needle-Felting Magic:
New Techniques, Creative Projects
© 2009 by Margo Duke

That Patchwork Place® is an imprint
of Martingale & Company®.

Martingale & Company
20205 144th Ave. NE
Woodinville, WA 98072-8478 USA
www.martingale-pub.com

Printed in China
14 13 12 11 10 09   8 7 6 5 4 3 2 1

Library of Congress Cataloging-in-Publication Data
Library of Congress Control Number: 2009020557

ISBN: 978-1-56477-919-9

Mission Statement
*Dedicated to providing quality products
and service to inspire creativity.*

Credits

President & CEO: Tom Wierzbicki

Editor in Chief: Mary V. Green

Managing Editor: Tina Cook

Developmental Editor: Karen Costello Soltys

Technical Editor: Nancy Mahoney

Copy Editor: Sheila Chapman Ryan

Design Director: Stan Green

Production Manager: Regina Girard

Illustrator: Laurel Strand

Cover & Text Designer: Regina Girard

Photographer: Brent Kane

Contents

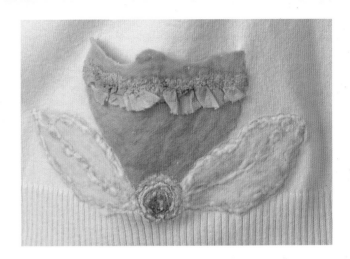

The Projects

Introduction

In this book, *Making More Needle-Felting Magic*, I've combined three of my passions—machine needle felting, free-motion stitching, and wet felting, mostly done in that order. You will find that stitching prior to wet felting adds lovely detail and an almost sculpted look that will enhance your work. When the wool shrinks as it is wet felted and fulled, the detail truly "pops."

When I began writing my first book, *Needle-Felting Magic* (Martingale & Company, 2007), machine needle felting was just beginning to make its mark in becoming one of the fastest growing artistic trends. I knew that once the secret was out, there would be no stopping the unleashed creativity. Since these machines were introduced to the market through local sewing-machine dealerships, they took a little while to catch on; sewers for the most part didn't quite know what to do with them. After all, as a sewer you know that there are patterns to follow and fabric to cut out, so it's more than a little confusing to have a machine with multiple needles but no thread, no pattern, and nothing telling you the type or size of the fabric you need to use. Once the machine was discovered by fiber artists, things started to change, and every sewing-machine manufacturer began jumping on the bandwagon due to the increased interest and demand.

The Internet has played a big part for those of us seeking inspiration and in providing us with the amazing ability to exchange ideas and interact with like-minded fiber artists from all over the world. If you spend time on the Internet, you'll find it quite amazing that many machine-needle-felting artists have developed a recognizable "stamp," making their style of work identifiable and clarifying that whatever art appreciation, skill, and training they developed in the past will most likely come through in the design and color interpretation of their work.

It's a natural progression to combine machine-needle and wet felting; it opens up a whole new vista for those of us enthralled with the felting process, because it allows more control over the fiber and provides the ability to add great detail. There are many great books on wet felting written by devoted and educated artists who have trailblazed the way for the rest of us. In that vein, while we want to ensure that the high standards for proper felting technique and quality are maintained, there is an opportunity to try new things using our needle-felting machines.

As part of that philosophy, I've deviated from some of the rules that are considered etched in stone; however, I hope you'll agree that the results are what matter. One of these rules is to never cut the wool roving and for the most part that is true—with a couple of exceptions. The first being "Lost in a Meadow Bag" on page 39, where the wool is purposely cut between color variations. When the pieces of wool are spread apart and placed correctly, they produce a painted effect, with the flat edges almost looking like brush strokes in places. The other exception is that when tiny snippets of wool are required for small buds or flowers, it's much easier to control the design when you work with a certain length.

In the quilting world there are those who do not use a sewing machine except for the piecing. All of the other work is done by hand, and indeed those quilts are very special and beautiful; however, for other prize-winning quilts, lots of gorgeous finishing work is done by machine. Machine quilting has gained both in popularity and respect and I think the same will happen for machine felting. In no way do I profess to be an expert felt maker; however, it's fun sharing my ideas and techniques.

Materials and Tools

*I*n this chapter, we'll review the basic materials and tools needed to create all of the projects—for specific materials, please see the individual projects. To find a source for the items listed below, see "Resources" on page 47.

Materials

Water-soluble fabric. For our purpose you will need water-soluble fabric, which is a different product than the water-soluble stabilizer you may be familiar with. Water-soluble fabric is white, *not* clear film, and feels like fabric.

Monofilament thread. In most of the projects you'll need to secure embellishments in place by using your sewing machine for free-motion stitching. For this step, I usually use Sulky or YLI clear polyester monofilament because I've found that it works especially well; whatever stitching pattern you choose will show and create texture while the actual stitches aren't as apparent.

Wool, silk, and other natural fibers. A wide array of variegated shades and fiber mixes all lend themselves particularly well to achieving the subtle palette of flower colors. I've used BFL wool fibers in several of the projects. BFL comes from Blue Faced Leicester sheep and is a luscious, incredibly soft wool fiber that felts well. Merino is another wonderful wool that is used in the fiber mix. Silk must be mixed with wool in order for it to felt.

Prefelt fabric. This felting fabric is factory-needled, short fiber wool that felts quickly and can also be cut into shapes to be incorporated into wet felting work. It can be purchased in various weights, colors, and sizes, and is sold by the sheet or yard. I've used it as a base layer for several of the projects in this book. Fine sheets of prefelt or "Felbi" can be layered to create a heavier fabric. Roving can be made into a prefelt by needle felting a length and using it for cut-out shapes. Prefelt does require additional felting because it doesn't have enough integrity in its original state to use as a fabric.

Wool fabric or felt. Using a good quality wool fabric base is an option if you simply want to machine needle felt and want to eliminate wet felting. Simply create the shapes as directed and needle felt them in place on your fabric selection; the only difference is you must completely rinse off any soap from your flower shapes before needle felting in place. You must also reduce any patterns that allow for shrinkage during the wet-felting process.

Tools for Needle Felting

Machine Needle Felting

- Needle-felting machine or sewing machine attachment (attachments are available only for certain brands—check with your sewing machine dealer)

- A bamboo stick, tweezers, or other "pointer" to save your fingers when machine needle felting

Hand Needle Felting

- Hand-needle-felting tool and needles

- Block of high-density foam at least 15" x 17" x 2"

Tools for Wet Felting

- Piece of bubble wrap (approximately 36" x 60") for larger pieces

- Small "pool noodle" (a foam flotation device used for swimming) for larger pieces

- Sushi or bamboo mat for smaller pieces

- Piece of nylon netting the same size as the project

- Old panty hose or rubber bands

- Dishwashing liquid soap

- Sponge

- Rowenta steam generator or a steam iron

Understanding Wet Felting and Fulling

When you needle felt using a machine or hand felting needles, the fibers are meshed by the needles "poking" them together; however, when you wet felt, the soap, water, and agitation work to interlock the fibers. The basic process for wet felting is to lay out three or four thin layers of wool wisps (if using prefelt for the base, the prefelt is considered one layer), making a crisscross of layers until the desired thickness is reached. Lay the fibers directly on the smooth side of the bubble wrap (or bamboo mat), and then cover the layers of fiber with a piece of nylon netting. This keeps the fibers from shifting. Gently wet the netting with a sponge using warm soapy water; it will penetrate into the wool. Press down the fiber and get all the air out as you gently rub in a circular motion with the palms of your hands. The soap allows your hands to glide smoothly, and the netting should feel slightly slippery; if it doesn't, add a little more liquid soap to your water. Don't overdo the soap, though, or it may impede the felting process. Remove the netting and carefully turn the piece over; replace the netting and rub the other side. You may need to wet it down some more and add more soap for this. With a little practice, you will get the feel of this.

Once the fibers are wet and secure you are going to roll them up. Place a pool noodle on one end of the bubble wrap. Roll the pool noodle, bubble wrap, fibers, and netting together and secure the roll. Next you are going to begin rolling the project using your hands. The felting time varies for this process; start with rolling 100 times. Then unwrap the roll, remove the netting, and rotate the piece 90°. Reroll the pieces and roll again for another 100 to 200 times. Keep unwrapping, rotating, and rolling until you see the fibers begin to meld together. Rotating helps the shrinkage to be more uniform on all sides. This process of rolling the felt back and forth in the bubble wrap causes the individual fibers to draw closer together, removing the air pockets and tightening the felt. You will be finished rolling your felt piece when it feels like a piece of fabric with no loose individual fibers and passes the "pinch test" (pinch some fiber between your fingers—if it lifts away from the rest of the fiber, it is not felted enough; pinching should lift the whole piece).

The final stage is the fulling or shrinking stage that tightens up and hardens the felt. This stage finishes your piece and is very satisfying and fun! After you felt a piece or two, your hands will get to know how the felt changes and feels as it hardens. There are other ways to accomplish this, but for this purpose, we'll squeeze out any excess water and, using both hands, throw the wad of felt into the sink or onto a hard surface. After a dozen or so throws, flatten out your felt and check it. Repeat the process of throwing and checking until the felt is hardened the desired amount. I've noticed that the properties change as the felt hardens; it actually seems to slightly "bounce."

If the felt is misshaped or an area needs to shrink a little more, use your hands to rub or roll the area with a bit more soapy water. You can gently stretch out areas of your felt that have shrunk a little too much, but be careful how you do this so it won't ripple. Using only the edge of your palm and a flat surface, push the felt in the direction you want it to go. Finally, rinse the felt well and lay flat to dry. Using a pressing cloth and steam iron set on the wool setting, steam the felt from the wrong side. (A steam generator is invaluable for this task.)

For the projects in this book, hardening the felt until it gets a pebbly appearance is important only for the bag or for other things that get lots of wear; for these projects, hardening is necessary for longevity and to avoid pilling. Some fibers are naturally more "hairy" after felting and require shaving to become smooth—we do not need to do this for any of our projects. Art Flower Felts on page 7 do not require as much work and are a very effective display of texture and color; these are more likely to be displayed than worn—we want them to shrink enough to attain their sculptural look but they don't need to be hardened (yes, I know I'm breaking the rules here again).

The Language of Flowers

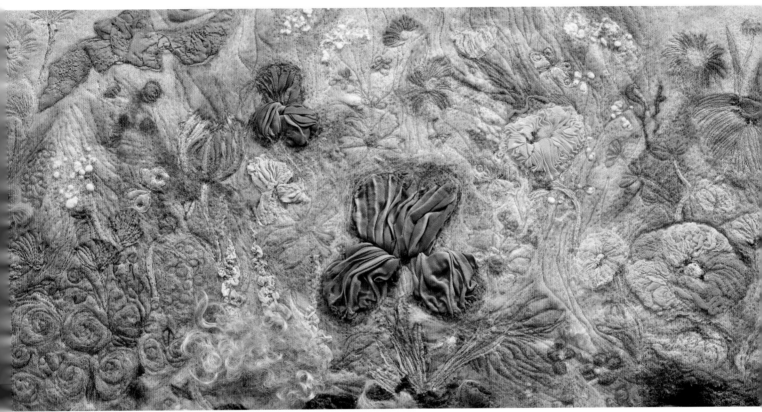

The Garden Party—flowers ready for the party, all dressed up in their needle-felted best!

What is so special about flowers? What is it about them that captures the imagination? Is it the promise of the fragrance to come or the pure delight in their beauty? Flowers are a part of everyday life and adorn everything from the clothing we wear to the home furnishings we surround ourselves with and the art we create. They are painted, stitched both with thread and ribbon, woven, felted, knitted, crocheted, and everything in between, and so it's natural that we would like to use our needle-felting machines to join in on the fun too.

Art Flower Felts

Art Flower Felts are simply felted flower pieces that provide an interesting way to showcase all the subtleties and shapes found in the garden. They are small enough to allow a focus on detail, and although they can be used alone for display, they will enhance any project that they are incorporated into. The discipline of really studying and mastering flower and petal shapes trains your eye to notice detail and develops your ability to add interest to your other projects as well.

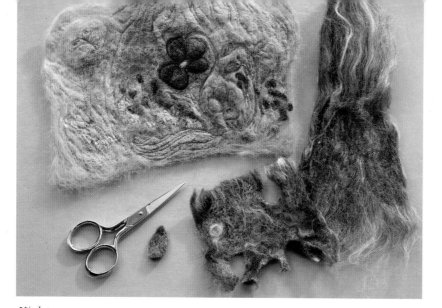

Violets

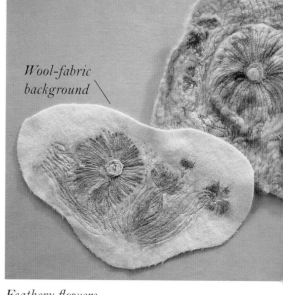

Wool-fabric background

Feathery flowers

Making Art Flower Felts

I began making these small Art Flower Felts when experimenting with combining machine needle felting and wet felting, and my results were so rewarding that I've continued along this garden path. For the purpose of this book, we will focus on the backgrounds, the general types of petals and flowers, and the method used for each type. Once mastered, these simple methods can be applied using your own individual taste. Remember, this is not an exact science but therein lies the excitement—you really don't know what the results will be until the process has been completed and you can see your piece transformed.

Here are a few tips to help you along your own garden path. I'd suggest that you begin with one variety of flower and study everything about that selection down to the finest detail. It may help to do a few sketches even if (like me!) you don't consider yourself able to draw well. Drawing helps you really focus on the color variations, shape, and properties of the flower petals, leaves, flower center, and stem. Are there multiple blooms bursting forth from one stem? Are the flowers low to the ground or towering? I believe studying and drawing has helped me toward my goal of training my eye and hands to create the illusion of a specific flower—and this is all about creating illusions! As with everything else, you will make great progress if you practice, and for us that only can mean one thing—lots of playing!

The Backgrounds

All of the flower backgrounds begin in the same way: a piece of water-soluble fabric a little larger than the size of your finished piece placed on the foam block with a mix of green wool fiber tacked in place using your hand-felting tool. Although fiber can be needle felted without using water-soluble fabric as a base, using it allows the edges of the finished piece to be finer, enabling a more delicate effect, and permits stitching over these thin areas. To add interest, add silk, mohair curls, yarns, or snippets of ribbon in colors that repeat the flower colors and enhance the overall effect. Even the tiniest snippets can create an interesting illusion of more flowers in the background, especially after stitching.

Machine needle felt the background before adding your flower and leaf choice and then, using monofilament thread, free-motion stitch over the entire piece. Cut away any excess water-soluble fabric and place your finished piece in a basin or sink with a little warm water to carefully dissolve the water-soluble fabric. Using some dishwashing liquid soap in your palms, gently rub the back and then the front with your palms about 100 times on each side. Rub any loose fibers extending beyond the edges toward the piece. Swish around in hot water, squeeze out, bunch up and throw the piece onto the sink about 100 to 200 times until it shrinks and the stitching becomes pronounced. Rinse well

Water-soluble background

Tulle petals and flowers

and blot with a towel. Lay flat to dry. Using a steam iron set on the wool setting, steam the pieces from the wrong side. I like to use my Rowenta Steam Generator—it is my other most favorite tool besides my Embellisher; I absolutely love it for my work. If you'd like to add more interest and texture, now is the time to add more needle felting, hand embroidery, or beads.

A Mélange of Flower Petals

There are a few easy ways to make flower petals or leaf shapes for some of your work, and most of these techniques are used for the projects in this book. Keep in mind that many of the flowers don't need to be wet felted if you only want to needle felt them; however, these same flowers do add wonderful detail when incorporated into wet felted projects too.

Violets: Machine needle felt a length of wool roving—for shading you can blend the colors and fiber mix. Cut out petal shapes before machine needle felting in place. Flowers such as violets, pansies, and daisies can easily be created using this method. Stitching details over and around these petal shapes prior to wet felting will produce exciting results once the project has gone through all the wet felting and fulling stages.

Daisies and other feathery flowers: Use feathery wisps of fiber, machine needle felt in place and add fine detail with free-motion machine stitching. Daisies, thistles, and fantasy flowers can be produced using this method, and they're great for backgrounds.

Tulips and black-eyed Susans: Cut short petal lengths of roving, separate into two or three pieces depending on how thick it is, and dip in soapy water. Blot on a towel and shape into a petal. I've been asked why the soap is necessary—it acts as a wetting agent and allows the water to penetrate the fibers and assists in keeping the shape. Experiment without the soap and you will see that the fiber does not stay wet long enough to be shaped. Hoop a piece of tulle and machine needle felt the petals, shaping more as you proceed (the tulle provides stabilization). Tear away the tulle before needle felting and stitching in place on your project. This is good for a multitude of flowers such as daisies, pansies, violets, and tulips. Combed fiber in variegated tones is especially effective for flowers such as tulips.

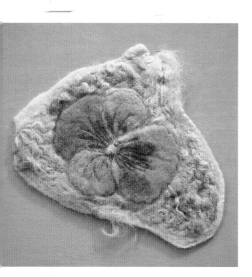

Pansy

Shibori iris and tulips

Pansies: Trace the pattern onto water-soluble fabric, machine needle felt the wool on top, and then simply cut off the excess water-soluble fabric. Needle felt in place on your project and stitch. There is no need to rinse at this point because the water-soluble fabric will dissolve during the wet felting process.

Shibori iris, tulips, and poppies: This technique uses pleated silk (see "Simple Shibori" on page 11) to create fabulous iris, tulip, poppy, and other blossoms. The fabric can be easily manipulated to form interesting curves and delicate shapes. The finer the silk, the easier it is on your needles.

Pansy pattern

Shibori flower materials

Shibori Flowers

Cut a length of shibori fabric or ribbon (see "Simple Shibori" at right). Pull it apart and carefully cut the corners, rounding them as shown. Save these tiny scraps to enhance the backgrounds of your Art Flower Felts.

To save your needles, *do not use the foot pedal initially*, but *turn the wheel by hand* and carefully needle felt only along the edge. Then use the foot pedal to secure the shibori flower in place *without moving the fabric;* it's only necessary to anchor the edges since it will be stitched to secure. Do a small section at a time. Once you have the desired effect, stitch in place.

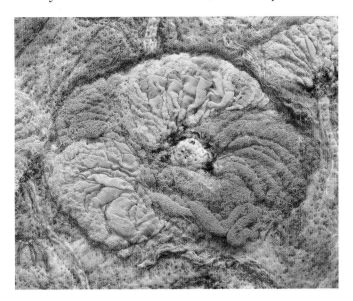

Poppy

Simple Shibori

Silk pleating adds another opportunity to create interesting shapes for flowers and leaves. Shibori encompasses many masterful stitching and pleating techniques developed in Japan centuries ago. It's a very beautiful form of textile art that appeals to artists and designers alike because there are endless stitching patterns, some with great meaning. There are several books on the topic, and it's well worth the effort to take a class to gain expertise through a hands-on experience.

For our purpose, we will focus on simple pleating. The traditional way of pleating is an art form in itself and even then, there are several ways to accomplish this. The silk is first dyed in a light shade, sometimes stitched, sometimes not, rolled around a PVC pole, then tightly wrapped using a cord or string much like a barber shop pole. The silk is wet, scrunched, and overdyed with a deeper color. It must be allowed to dry completely before removing the cord or twine in order for the pleats to remain. You'll be left with a two-tone piece of pleated fabric, one color inside the pleat and another on the top of the pleat. Since we need only very small amounts for our work, we can either purchase ready-made ribbon or fabric (see "Resources" on page 47) or we can make our own using a rolling pin!

In the version I've developed for my flowers, I can have a colorful variety of pleated silk on hand with very little work and a lot of satisfaction when the gorgeous pleats are unveiled. The rolling pin I use for this purpose is marble and very smooth, making it easy for the silk to be "scrunched." You may have to practice if you are using another type of rolling pin.

Using Colorhue Dye, dye a piece of silk no wider than your rolling pin in a soft shade. This first dyeing should be a light color and the overdying a darker shade. Lay the fabric flat on a table, place the rolling pin on one end, and begin rolling the fabric onto the rolling pin. If the rolling pin isn't slippery enough, spray a cloth with silicon, wipe the rolling pin, and then thoroughly wipe it off. (Keep the rolling pin for this use only and do **NOT** use it for baking.) Use masking tape to tape the fabric to the rolling pin at one end (A) and to itself at the other end (B). This end needs to move freely when pushed up. Tie a piece of cord or twine to end A on the rolling pin and begin wrapping around the fabric every ¼" or ½" until you reach end B. Secure this end of cord by turning it around in the same place a few times and tying a knot.

Push the fabric toward end A as far as possible. If it's difficult to move, sometimes spraying the fabric with water will help.

Push to create tight pleats.

Once the fabric is scrunched as much as possible, wet it thoroughly by soaking it in a bucket or sink. Remove the rolling pin from the bucket (or sink) and blot any excess water with an old towel. Place the rolling pin over a tub and pour the deeper dye color over the scrunched fabric, turning as you go to make sure the color is even. Blot on a towel and leave overnight to dry thoroughly. Remove the cord or twine and unroll the fabric. Note that water will remove the pleats; however, an interesting striped pattern will remain.

If you don't care to get into dyeing but want to practice the pleating, just use a silk scarf or other suitable fabric that has already been dyed and forego the over-dyeing. It will just be one color—but it will still be gorgeous and useful for a myriad of flower or background shapes.

We Want Glitz!

Glitzy Confection is fiber enhanced with glitter dust. Although it can't be wet felted, it can be added to a project after it's wet felted, and then needle felted or stitched in place. A little Glitzy Confection goes a long way and will enhance many of your Art Flower Felts and other projects. Of course, you can always use Angelina fiber, however, I've found a simple and fun way to have an ample supply of Glitzy Confection on hand to create butterflies and other details for the backgrounds.

Spread out a wispy layer of fiber over the shiny side of a piece of freezer paper; the fibers can be wool, silk, or any fiber mix. Sprinkle this fiber mix *lightly* with a 50/50 mix of textile medium and water. (Too much textile medium will cause a plastic-type coating.) Place a piece of tulle over the fibers while they're still wet and pat to even everything out. Remove the tulle, sprinkle the fibers very lightly with glitter, and leave until dry—usually several hours or overnight—before peeling the Glitzy Confection from the freezer paper. This works best when coordinating the colorway of the fiber and the glitter; light glitter with light colors and deeper tones of glitter with darker fiber. In order to needle felt this Glitzy Confection, tear off pieces as you want to use them. You will need to veil the Glitz by placing a very fine, almost invisible wisp of roving over it. You can also cut out butterfly wings to stitch in place.

Rolling pin shibori

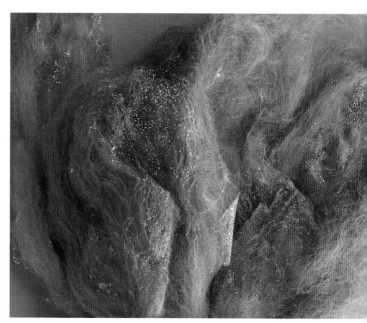

Glitzy Confection

Tulip Pockets

Enhance a simple cardigan with these cheerful tulip pockets.

Finished pocket size:
approximately 3¼" x 6" with leaves

Materials

Yields two tulip pockets.

2 pieces, 8" x 10", of water-soluble fabric

½ ounce of mixed soft coral and peach merino wool roving for tulips

½ ounce of soft green merino wool roving for leaves

1 yard of variegated green yarn for leaf veins

10" of variegated ribbon or yarn for pinwheel flower

2 pieces, 1" x 6", of Hanah variegated hand-dyed ribbon for tulip embellishment

Nylon netting, approximately 8" x 8"

Clear polyester monofilament and/or coordinating thread

Hand-needle-felting tool

2"-thick foam block

Bamboo mat

Small mesh bag

Cardigan sweater or other garment (optional)

Tulip material mix

Large pinwheel flower

Instructions

1. Using the tulip pattern on page 15, trace the tulip shape onto each piece of water-soluble fabric. Cut out, leaving a 1" border around each tulip.

2. Place a traced tulip on the foam block. Allowing it to extend beyond the pattern shape, lay wisps of roving in three layers over the tulip in a crisscross manner as follows:
   Layer one: horizontal
   Layer two: vertical
   Layer three: horizontal

❦ *Felting Snippet* ❧

Temporarily cover the roving with a piece of nylon netting while machine needle felting to avoid needle breakage.

3. Using a hand-needle-felting tool, tack the roving in place, and then machine needle felt the entire tulip. Make two tulips.

4. Using monofilament thread in your sewing machine, stitch vertical lines on each tulip, machine needle felt along one edge of the hand-dyed ribbon, and then stitch the hand-dyed ribbon to the tulip on the line indicated.

5. Repeat steps 1–3 to make the leaves. Make four leaves.

6. Using the lines on the pattern as a guide, machine needle felt the variegated yarn onto each leaf. Using monofilament thread in your sewing machine, stitch the veins on the leaves.

7. At the sink and using warm water, gently rinse off the water-soluble fabric from the pieces.

8. Lay the two tulips and four leaves on a bamboo mat and cover with netting, wet with soapy water, and rub gently for a couple of minutes. Roll everything up, secure the ends with rubber bands, and begin rolling. After a few minutes, unroll and remove the netting. Rotate the pieces and roll again. Continue in this manner until it passes the pinch test. Carefully rinse in warm soapy water and place in a small mesh bag; throw it in the sink about 50 times to shrink and harden. Refer to "Understanding Wet Felting and Fulling" on page 6 for more details as needed. Rinse thoroughly. Leave until dry. Use a pressing cloth and steam iron set on the wool setting to steam the pieces from the wrong side.

9. Position the tulips on the cardigan sweater and hand baste in place. Using monofilament thread in your sewing machine, stitch around the sides and bottom of each tulip, leaving the top open.

10. Place the leaves at the bottom of the tulip as shown in the placement guide on page 15; hand baste in place. Machine stitch around each leaf using monofilament thread.

11. Twist the variegated ribbon or yarn between your forefinger and thumb to form a spiral, creating a large pinwheel flower. Machine needle felt it onto a piece of heavy netting. Tear away the excess netting and machine stitch the flower in place between the leaves.

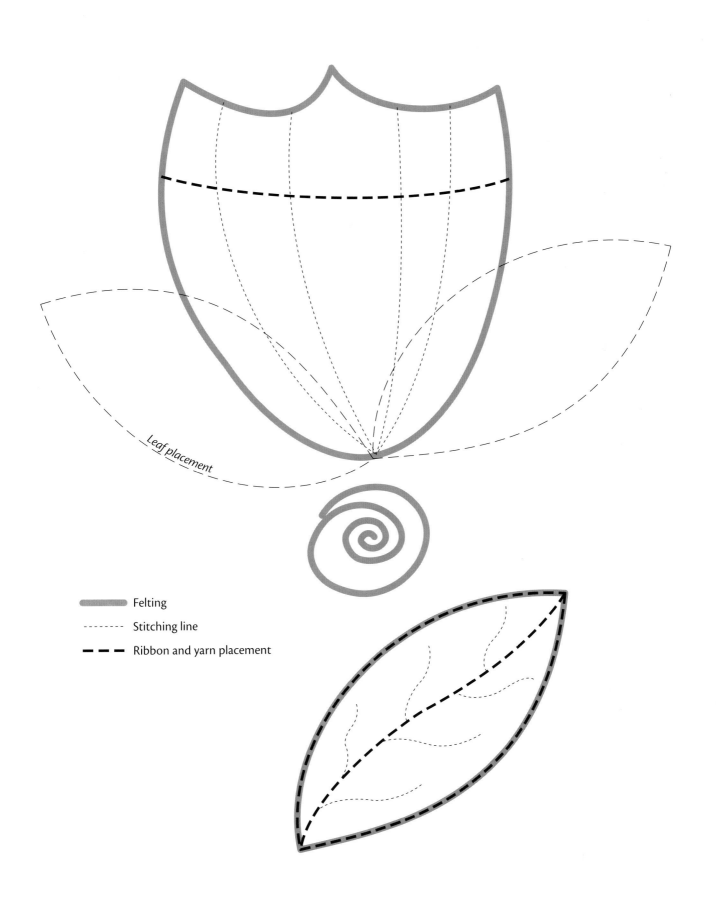

Leaf placement

Felting

Stitching line

Ribbon and yarn placement

Flower Fairy Lampshade

Finished Size: 5" x 14" x 11"

*This light and
airy confection
looks lovely adorning
an accent lamp.*

Materials

5" x 14" x 11" self-adhesive craft lampshade

¼ yard of water-soluble fabric

3 to 5 silk hankies in cinnamon color*

¼ yard of silk gauze in color similar to hankies

¼ yard of fabric in color similar to hankies to
   cover the lampshade base

Clear polyester monofilament thread

Hand-needle-felting tool

2"-thick foam block

Textile medium

Glitter

Craft glue (I like Aileen's Tack-It Over
   and Over)

   *These can be dyed easily with Colorhue Dye
   (See "Resources" on page 47).*

Instructions

1. Remove the adhesive cover from the
   lampshade and use it as a pattern to trace
   the shape onto the water-soluble fabric; or
   use the pattern on page 18. *Do not cut out.*

2. Use the lampshade pattern to cut out the cover fabric and press it onto the lampshade, following the manufacturer's instructions. Set the lampshade base aside.

3. Place the water-soluble fabric on the foam block. Carefully lay the silk hankies over the pattern shape, aligning the hankies along the top and sides of the pattern (overlapping is fine) and allowing the bottom to dip slightly in places. Beginning in the center and working toward the outer edges, use your hand-needle-felting tool to tack the hankies in place, and then completely machine needle felt the entire piece. Using monofilament thread in your sewing machine, free-motion stitch over the entire piece—the stitching pattern doesn't matter too much since it won't show.

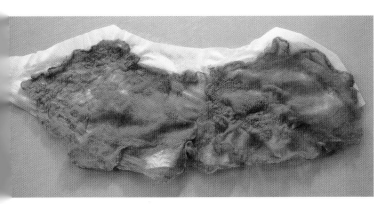

Place hankies on water-soluble fabric.

4. Cut the silk gauze twice the length and double the height of the lampshade pattern. Fold in half lengthwise and press the fold. Cut along the open edges to make points.

Folded gauze cut into points.

5. Working on the foam block and using the hand-needle-felting tool, begin tacking the gauze to the top of the hankie piece, starting at one end. Use your index finger to create pleats, tacking in place as you go. Carefully machine needle felt along the top edge and needle felt again about 1" down from the top edge.

Create pleats along the top of the gauze.

6. Using monofilament thread in your sewing machine, free-motion stitch along both needle-felted areas in a small figure-eight design as shown.

Stitch along the top of the gauze through the pleats.

7. Carefully cut away the excess water-soluble fabric. Rinse in warm water and blot with an old towel. Pour half of the bottle of textile medium into your palm and squeeze it through the lampshade. Place on a flat surface, *lightly* sprinkle with glitter, and let dry.

8. To finish, glue the top (stitched portion) of the lampshade to the lampshade base. Use tiny dabs of glue to close the back opening.

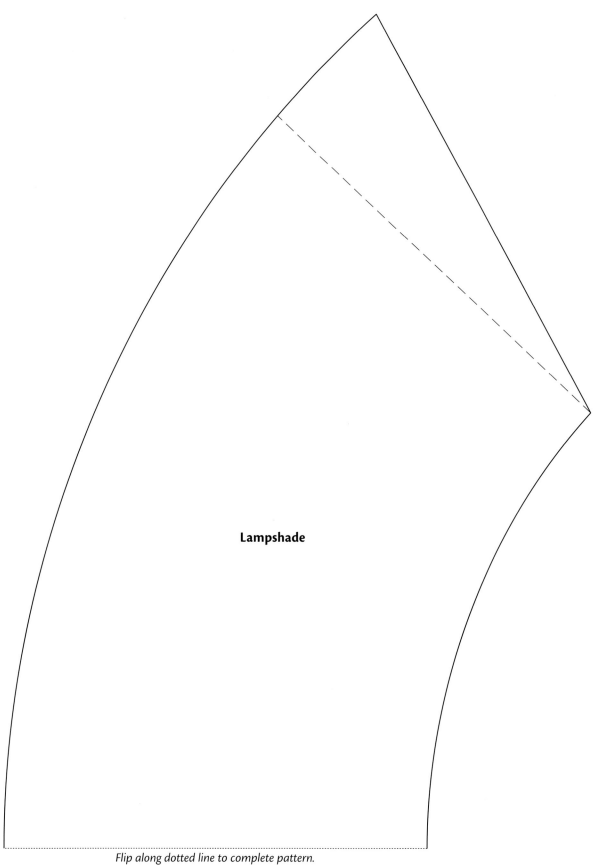

Lampshade

Flip along dotted line to complete pattern.

Painterly Pillow

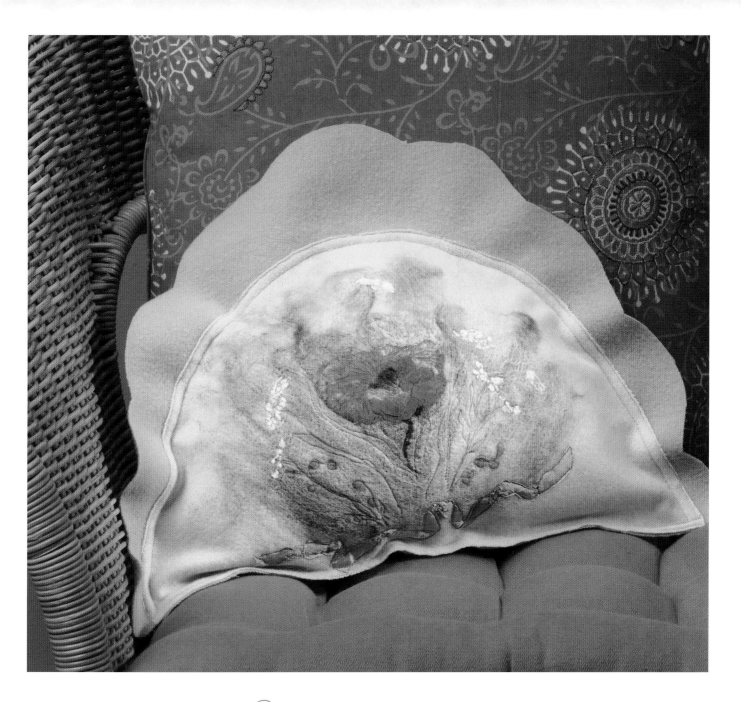

*This elegant but easy pillow can
showcase your Art Flower Felts.*

Finished size: 16" x 11"

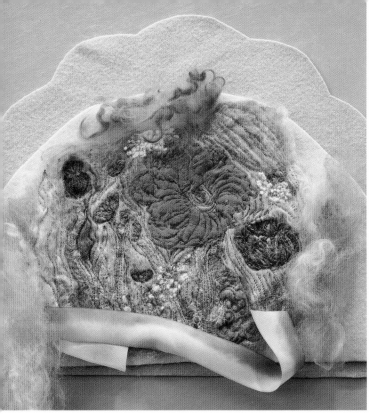

Select the fiber mix to blend with the background of your Art Flower Felt.

Materials

1 piece, 10" x 15", of pale pink wool fabric or wool felt for pillow front

1 piece, 13" x 17", of sage green wool fabric or wool felt for pillow back

13"-long piece of hand-dyed silk ribbon in a color to enhance the Art Flower Felts selection (optional)

Small amount of silk and/or wool roving fibers in colors to match the Art Flower Felts selection

Choice of Art Flower Felts (see page 7)

⅜ yard of muslin for pillow insert

Polyester fiberfill

Clear polyester monofilament and/or coordinating thread

Tracing paper

Instructions

1. Trace the patterns on pages 21 and 22 onto tracing paper and cut out. (Be sure to enlarge the pillow-back pattern.) Use the paper patterns to cut out one pale pink pillow front and one sage green pillow back.

2. Selecting colors of roving that will help blend your Art Flower Felts into the background, machine needle felt the roving in soft feathers around the center area where your Art Flower Felt selection will be. Make sure to use a light touch—you can always add more as you go along.

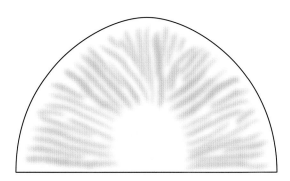

3. Place your Art Flower Felts in the center of the pillow front and pin in place. Machine needle felt in place, beginning near the center and working your way out; do not stitch over the flowers themselves, but rather just needle felt around them or you may ruin the textured effect you've created.

4. If desired, arrange the hand-dyed ribbon slightly over the Art Flower Felt at the bottom of your pillow front; pin. Using monofilament thread in your sewing machine, free-motion stitch on top of the ribbon.

5. Use the paper pattern for the pillow front to cut out two pieces of muslin. Stitch the muslin pieces together using a ¼" seam allowance, leaving a 3" opening at the bottom to add the fiberfill. Stuff the muslin pillow form with the fiberfill and stitch the opening closed.

6. Center the pillow front on top of the pillow back, wrong sides together and aligning the bottom edges. Pin in place.

7. Machine stitch around the edge of the pillow front, leaving an opening at the bottom large enough to insert in the muslin form. Topstitch around the top of the pillow front again, ¼" from the edge.

8. Insert the muslin pillow form and machine stitch close to the edge to close the opening. Topstitch ¼" from the bottom edge, holding the pillow as flat as possible.

Pillow front
Cut 1 from pale pink wool
and 2 from muslin.

Place on fold.

Pillow back
Enlarge pattern 110%.
Cut 1 from sage green wool.

Place on fold.

Tea Party Cozy

Serve your tea in romantic style. Learn new techniques while creating a functional yet beautiful addition for your home—a perfect gift for a friend or yourself.

Finished size after felting: 13" x 11"
(to fit a large teapot—adjust for smaller size)
Size before felting: 16¼" x 13¾"

Materials

2 yards of lightweight white prefelt fabric

4 ounces of BFL/Merino wool roving mix in soft apple green for background

2 ounces of BFL/Merino wool roving mix in medium French blue for petals

1 sheet of Mulberry paper in Olive or deep green for background

½ yard of 1"-wide hand-dyed ribbon in variegated pink/plums for flower center

2 strips, 3" x 22", of silk gauze or chiffon in a soft green for side ruffle

Small bits of silk ribbon or other fiber in green and blue colors for petals

1 yard of 36"-wide water-soluble fabric

Clear polyester monofilament thread

Hand-needle-felting tool

2"-thick foam block

½ yard of nylon netting

Dark pencil

Bubble wrap

Pool noodle

Old panty hose

Small amount of dishwashing liquid

Instructions

1. Enlarge the pattern on page 26 and trace it onto the water-soluble fabric using a dark pencil, making sure you have a 2" margin on all sides. *Do not cut out.*

2. Lay half of the water-soluble pattern on the foam block, pencil side down. (We will be working half of the pattern at a time.) Fold the prefelt in half and trim it 2" larger than the pattern all around; place the double-thick prefelt on top of the entire pattern.

3. Cover the first half of the pattern and prefelt with a horizontal layer of apple green wool wisps; tack in place using your hand-needle-felting tool. The fiber wisps should extend slightly beyond the lines (you will cut out the pattern later). Cover the first layer with a vertical layer and tack in place using your hand-needle-felting tool. Ensure that the entire area is evenly covered.

4. Move the first half aside and repeat step 3 for the second half of the pattern.

5. Beginning at the center and working toward the outer edges, machine needle felt the entire piece.

6. For the six blue petals, machine needle felt the blue roving to create a prefelt; add bits of silk ribbon or other fiber as you needle felt. Using the petal shape on the pattern as a guide, cut out six petal shapes.

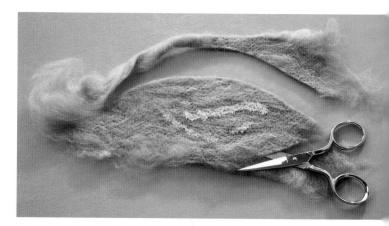

Flower petals embellished and cut.

7. Lay the petals around the top center as shown on the pattern; tack in place, and then completely machine needle felt the petals.

8. Tear the Mulberry paper into very fine pieces and strips. Place the Mulberry pieces on the green background. Add a few very fine wisps of apple green roving over the pieces as a veil (the paper resists needle felting). Tack in place and machine needle felt.

9. Twist the variegated ribbon between your forefinger and thumb to form a spiral, creating a large pinwheel flower. Machine needle felt it onto a piece of netting as shown in the "Tulip

Pockets" photo on page 13. Tear away the excess netting, center the pinwheel flower on the petals, and tack in place.

10. Beginning with the pinwheel flower center and using monofilament thread in your sewing machine, free-motion stitch the pinwheel center and around each petal, adding petal detail. Stitch over the Mulberry paper pieces and the background to mimic leafy growth.

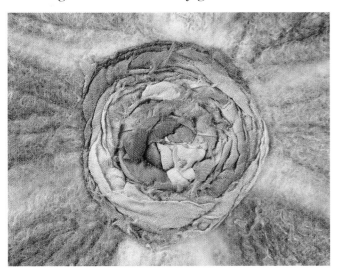

Top of Tea Party Cozy, pinwheel flower.

11. Cut out the pattern, cutting on the pencil line. At the sink and using warm water, gently allow the water-soluble fabric to dissolve. Add some dishwashing liquid to your hands and begin gently rubbing the tea cozy front and back between your hands to begin the wet-felting process. Lay the tea cozy on a piece of bubble wrap and cover with netting. Place a pool noodle on one end of the bubble wrap. Roll everything up, secure the ends with cut-off panty-hose legs, and tie in a bow (this will make untying easier); begin rolling. After a few minutes, unroll and remove the netting. Rotate the pieces and roll again. Continue in this manner until it passes the pinch test. Carefully rinse in warm soapy water and throw it in the sink 200 to 250 times until it shrinks and hardens. Refer to "Understanding Wet Felting and Fulling" on page 6 for more details as needed. The stitching detail will become pronounced. Rinse thoroughly and lay flat to dry. When dry, steam from the wrong side.

12. On the back of the tea cozy, machine needle felt the silk gauze strips along the *inside* edge of each side, allowing them to gather. Fold the tea cozy in half, wrong sides together, sandwiching the ruffle between the two layers. Machine stitch the front and back together along each side edge.

Sandwich the silk gauze ruffle between the front and back along each side.

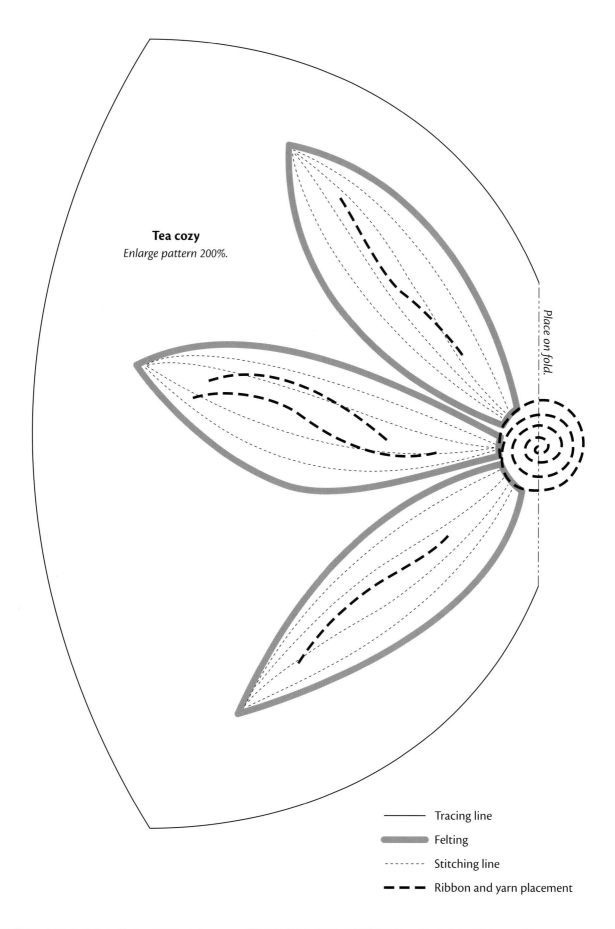

Tea cozy
Enlarge pattern 200%.

Place on fold.

Tracing line

Felting

Stitching line

Ribbon and yarn placement

This is a wonderfully creative way to mimic broken china mosaics without the mess—use your needle-felting machine, wool, and your own imagination to create gifts and decorations for your home. A sweet "Home" plaque announces how much you care for your home! And how about a "Welcome" or "Baby" plaque?

Finished size: approximately 9½" x 12"

Materials

1 piece, 11" x 15", of soft beige or natural shade of heavyweight prefelt fabric

2 ounces of natural or white wool roving (BFL is a good choice) for background

1 piece, 6" x 9", of vibrant blue lightweight prefelt fabric for lettering

Tiny bits of wool and/or yarns in color mix of your choice for "china" flowers

Small piece of aqua wool, machine needle felted and cut into a heart shape

Glass beads or buttons of various sizes in jewel tones

¼ ounce of white wool roving for hanger

15" length of coat-hanger wire for hanger

White florist's tape

Clear polyester monofilament thread

Hand-needle-felting tool

2"-thick foam block

Bamboo mat and bubble wrap

Pool noodle

Old panty hose

Nylon netting, approximately 10" x 12"

Fabric glue (optional)

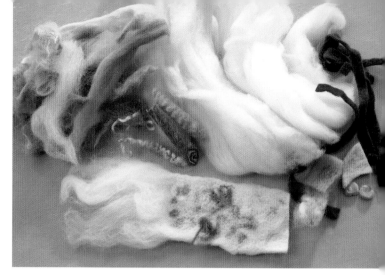

Material mix

Instructions

1. Referring to the layout guide below, cut a curve along the top edge of the 11" x 15" beige prefelt.

2. Lay the trimmed prefelt on the foam block and place wisps of natural or white roving around the top, sides, and bottom, leaving an approximately 3½" x 9" area in the center uncovered. Use the hand-needle-felting tool to tack the roving in place.

3. Divide the center area into four equal sections and, using the hand-needle-felting tool, temporarily tack pieces of yarn to divide the sections.

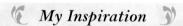

My Inspiration

This felt plaque is a replication of an actual broken china plaque that adorns the entrance of our home. I was fortunate enough to take a mosaic rug class from Turkish rug makers Mehmet Girgic and Theresa May O'Brien and I used their prefelt tile technique to effectively add the word "Home" to this felt plaque.

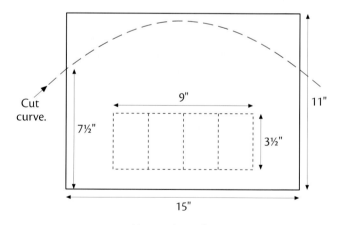

Home plaque layout

4. Cut the vibrant blue prefelt into tiles approximately ⅜" x ⅝". Dip the tiles in soapy water and create the *HOME* letters as shown in the project photo on page 27.

Placing the first letter

5. Dip the aqua heart in soapy water and hand needle felt in place as shown in the project photo.

6. To create the "china" plate edges for the top of your plaque, start by machine needle felting a long piece of white roving. Turn the thin edges under to make the edges smooth and to make the piece an even thickness. Add tiny bits of roving in assorted colors, including green for leaves, and machine needle felt them. Keep in mind that we are trying to mimic delicate china, so use tiny pieces. You will stitch over these later, so use basic flower and leaf shapes. Don't be concerned if they don't look realistic; we're simply creating an illusion.

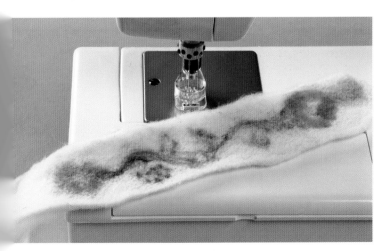

Creating the "broken china" border

7. Cut the "china" plate edge into pieces about 1" wide. Dip them in soapy water and place around the top as indicated. Tack these in place using the hand-needle-felting tool.

Placing the elements

8. At this point, machine needle felt all the pieces you have tacked in place. Machine needle felt in groups as you go along to help you remember what area has been machined.

9. Add some green irregular pieces of roving to resemble green glass as shown in the project photo. Make a piece of prefelt using a piece of green roving, machine needle felt it, and then cut it into irregularly shaped pieces. Place these beneath the aqua heart.

10. Create more "china" pieces in the same manner as you did in step 6, except cut these pieces into more irregular "broken china" shapes. Fill in the remaining areas mosaic style, leaving spaces between the shapes to resemble the grout. To add some interest, randomly add a few other colors by machine needle felting them to make a prefelt that you can cut into irregular pieces of your choice. Remember to dip each piece into soapy water before tacking in place. Make sure that everything has been machine needle felted in place before going on to the next step.

11. At the sewing machine, free-motion stitch around every tile (including the letters) using monofilament thread. The tiles will become more pronounced once wet felted. Free-motion stitch around some of the flower and leaf colors to enhance the detail and create a sculpted effect once wet felted.

12. Lay the plaque on a piece of bubble wrap and cover with a piece of netting; wet with soapy water and rub gently for a couple of minutes. Place a pool noodle on one end of the bubble wrap and roll everything up, secure the ends with cut-off panty-hose legs, and tie in a bow (this will make untying easier); begin rolling. After a few minutes, unroll and remove the netting. Rotate the plaque and roll again. Continue in this manner until it passes the pinch test. Rinse in warm soapy water and throw it in the sink about 100 times until it shrinks and hardens. Check often to manipulate if it seems to be misshapen. Refer to "Understanding Wet Felting and Fulling" on page 6 for more details as needed. Rinse thoroughly. Lay flat to dry. Using a pressing cloth and steam iron set on the wool setting, steam the plaque from the wrong side.

13. To make the hanger, place a length of white roving on the bamboo mat (a bamboo mat works best to harden the cord). Cover the wire with florist's tape. Wet the wool and fold it over the wire. Roll it very gently between your hands until it begins to take shape around the wire. Pull the excess off the ends. Once it begins to felt, fold the edge of the bamboo mat over the cord and roll, gently at first, and then with more strength as it begins to harden. The ends will

taper. Cords always appear harder when wet so don't stop too soon. When you think it is hard enough with no cracks, rinse it in hot soapy water and rub with your hands, rolling it in the mat some more. When hard, rinse thoroughly and leave to dry. When dry, bend the cord in the shape of the plaque. Place the cord on the back of the plaque as shown and hand stitch about 5" on each end to secure and stabilize the cord. Sew or glue the beads to the plaque to your liking.

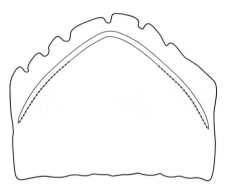

Hand stitch ends to secure.

Create a peaceful illusion on your table with your
Water Lily Hot Pad—it's both beautiful and functional.
This project is a fun way to try out different felting techniques!

Finished size: approximately 13" diameter

Materials

1 square, 16" x 16", of water-soluble fabric

2 squares, 15" x 15", of lightweight dark green prefelt fabric

2 ounces of deep green wool roving for lily pad

1 ounce of variegated deep green wool roving for lily pad

½ ounce of variegated yellowish green silk fiber for lily pad

10" square of leafy green silk velvet for background leaves

¼ yard of pink silk for water lily flower

Tiny amount of yellow wool roving for flower center

Clear polyester monofilament thread

Dark pencil

Hand-needle-felting tool

2"-thick foam block

Bubble wrap

Nylon netting, approximately 15" x 15"

Pool noodle

Old panty hose

Instructions

1. Using a dark pencil, draw a 14½" circle on the water-soluble fabric and mark the center of the circle.

2. Lay the water-soluble fabric on the foam block. Stack the two squares of dark green prefelt on top of the water-soluble fabric.

3. Lay out wisps of the deep green wool roving horizontally on top of the prefelt, and then place wisps vertically. Use the hand-needle-felting tool to tack the roving in place all over.

4. Lay out wisps of the variegated deep green roving, radiating out from the center to the edges. The easiest way to do this is to divide the circle into pie-shaped wedges and fill in each wedge, tacking with the hand tool as you go along. This placement will allow your pad to ripple slightly at the edges after wet felting.

5. Machine needle felt the entire piece. Cut out the circle, making the edges very slightly scalloped.

6. Following the illustration, needle felt long, thin strips of the yellowish green silk fiber along the lines indicated. This step will be easier if you dip each piece in soapy water before needle felting in place.

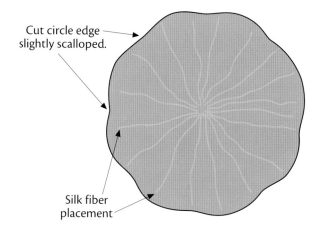

Cut circle edge slightly scalloped.

Silk fiber placement

7. Once everything has been completely needle felted, use monofilament thread in your sewing machine to free-motion stitch through the silk lines.

8. Enlarge the pattern on page 34, and then use it to cut out the background leaves from the leafy green velvet. Center the leaves on the lily pad and, using monofilament thread in your sewing machine, stitch around the edges and on each line as shown in the photo on page 33.

Velvet leaves stitched in place

9. Using the flower pattern, cut out one large flower and one small flower from the pink silk. Center the large flower on top of the green velvet leaves, rotating the flower so you can still see the leaves; stitch in the same manner as the leaves. Repeat with the small pink flower.

10. For the flower center, wet and roll the yellow roving between your palms to create five or six small, short "spikes." Place these in the center, the spikes facing toward the top of the water lily as shown in the photo below. Use the hand-needle-felting tool to tack in place, and then stitch in place using monofilament thread.

Yellow spikes for lily center

11. Lay the water lily pad on a piece of bubble wrap and cover with a piece of netting; wet with soapy water and rub gently for a couple of minutes. Place a pool noodle on one end of the bubble wrap and roll everything up, secure the ends with cut-off panty-hose legs, and tie in a bow (this makes untying easier); begin rolling. After a few minutes, unroll and remove the netting. Rotate the piece and roll again. (Remember your water lily should have a circular shape.) Continue in this manner until it passes the pinch test. Rinse in hot soapy water and throw it in the sink 100 to 200 times until it shrinks and hardens. Refer to "Understanding Wet Felting and Fulling" on page 6 for more details as needed. Rinse thoroughly. Gently pull around the edge of the circle to create slightly wavy edges that resemble a lily pad. Place on a flat surface to dry. Use a pressing cloth and steam iron set on the wool setting to steam the lily pad from the wrong side.

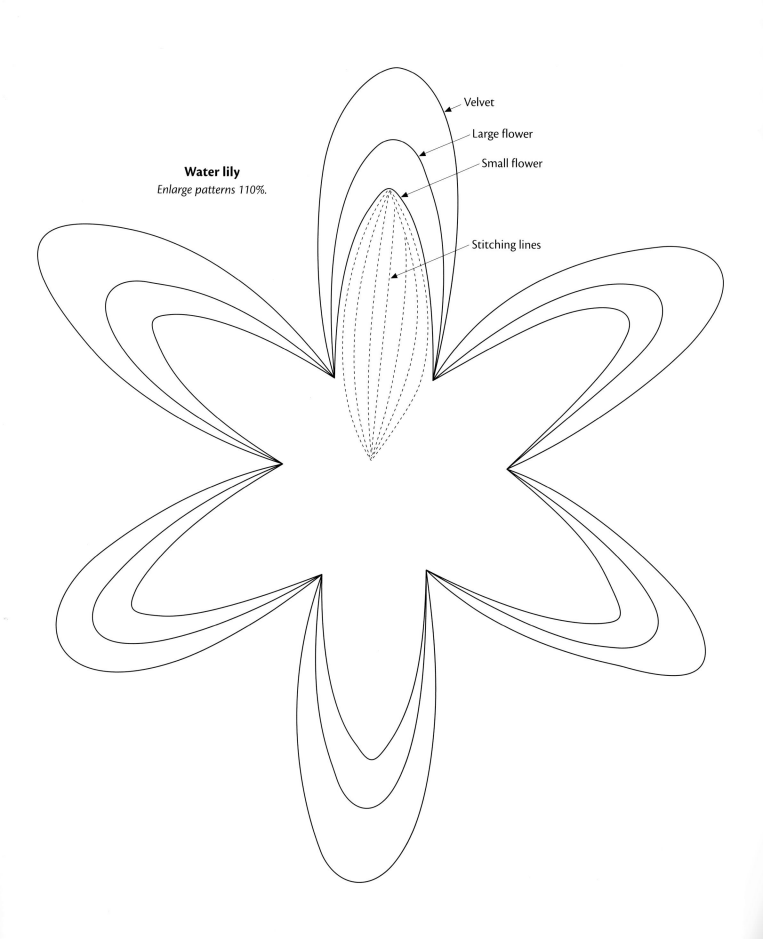

Water lily
Enlarge patterns 110%.

Velvet

Large flower

Small flower

Stitching lines

Leafy Rose Wrap

We'll be breaking all the rules in creating this light and airy elegant rose wrap. Whoever heard of needle felting silk gauze and throwing it in the washing machine to felt? But when you're done, you'll almost be able to smell the roses' perfume!

Materials

1 piece, 22" x 64", of deep leafy green silk gauze; do NOT remove the selvage along one side

4 ounces of wool-and-silk roving mix in vibrant variegated pink for roses

5 yards of thick-and-thin deep green yarn to match the gauze for vine

1 ounce of wool merino fiber in variegated woodrose color for vine

1 ounce of wool roving in deep green for leaves

Clear polyester monofilament thread

Hand-needle-felting tool

2"-thick foam block

Small amount of dishwashing liquid

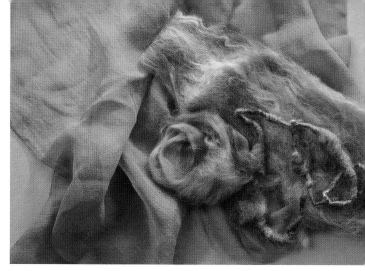
Material selection for wrap

Make a Sample Piece First

For this project it is highly recommended that you make a 10" sample using the same materials and techniques you'll use for the wrap. You'll learn quite a bit from this exercise: how much will the rose and yarn shrink? Do the roses provide the effect you want in your finished wrap? Are they too large or too small? How much will the material mix shrink in the process? From the information garnered you can adjust the rose size and/or placement as well as adjust the elements and yarn placement. When searching for just the right rose color don't look for the color "rose," because it might be too subdued. Instead, look for more vibrant colors, such as a variegated strawberry, which will have a more pleasing effect especially when paired with a deep, leafy green.

Instructions

1. On the long raw edge of the silk gauze, fold over 2" and press to make a hem; leave the sides raw. The selvage edge will be the bottom of your wrap. Along the folded edge, fold the silk gauze into quarters lengthwise and press the folds. The crease marks should be about 1" to 2" long.

2. Machine needle felt a long piece of the pink variegated roving; turn in any thin edges as you go to make it an even thickness.

3. Using the petal pattern on page 38, cut out the petals following the length of the fiber direction. Slightly pull the upper part of the petal very gently. If it is too thin and comes apart, simply needle felt more fiber underneath the petal and cut off the excess. You'll need five petals for each rose, 25 petals total. Save all of the scraps to use later.

Rose components

4. Referring to the photo below, place five petals on the foam block, overlapping them as shown. Use the hand-needle-felting tool to tack the petals in place. Use some of the leftover scraps to form a center for the rose and tack in place using a single hand-felting needle. Avoiding the center, machine needle felt the rose carefully, securing all the petals together. Selectively place the needles in the flower center and needle felt in place. Continue selectively needle felting until all the rose pieces are secure—they don't have to be flattened at this point. Make a total of five roses.

Completed rose

5. Center the folded edge of the silk gauze on the foam block with the raw edge of the hem facing *up*. We'll be working on one section at a time. Place your largest rose on the center mark, down just a little from the folded edge, and use your hand-needle-felting tool to tack it in place. Referring to the placement guide on page 38 as needed, place a rose on each crease mark, and then at each end of the wrap, leaving no seam allowance.

6. Lay thin wisps of woodrose fiber along the long raw edge, slightly above and below to cover the raw edge. With the hand-needle-felting tool, tack the fiber in place as you go along to secure. Don't be concerned about the needles "pulling" the gauze since this part will shrink up during felting.

7. Create small roses from the leftover pink scraps by shaping them into buds and poking the fiber in place with a single felting needle on the foam block. Center a rosebud halfway between the large roses, on top of the woodrose fiber, and tack in place with the hand-needle-felting tool.

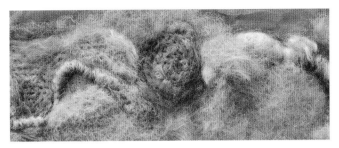

Small rosebuds

8. On the foam block, use the green yarn to swag between the small rosebud to the large roses on either side and tack in place using the hand-needle-felting tool. For the leaves, machine needle felt a length of green roving, and then cut out leaf shapes of your choice. Add the leaves and more scraps of the rose material to mimic small buds and leaves.

9. Very carefully, machine needle felt the complete section, including the roses again and all the rose centers so they can be stitched. For each remaining section of the wrap, repeat steps 7 and 8, and then machine needle felt each section.

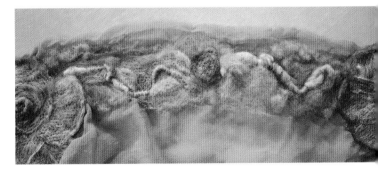

Vine and rosebud placement

10. With monofilament thread in your sewing machine, free-motion stitch the entire machine-needle-felted part of the wrap. Stitch around the rose petals and rose centers, creating definition; stitch over the yarns and around the rosebuds and leaves as well.

11. Once stitching is completed, set your washer to the gentle cycle, with a "hot wash, cool rinse" setting. Place the wrap in the washing machine and fill with hot water, adding a very small amount of dishwashing soap. When the washing machine stops, remove your wrap and give the roses the pinch test. If they need a little more felting, continue rubbing them at a sink until they pass the pinch test. Once they pass the test, swish your wrap in warm soapy water, squeeze out the excess water, bunch up the wrap, and throw it against the sink about 100 to 200 times until the fibers have shrunk and the stitching is more pronounced. Rinse well and place on a flat surface to dry. Using a steam iron set on the silk setting, steam the gauze and roses from the wrong side.

12. On each end, gather the raw edges in 1" pleats and secure behind the end rose on each side with a few machine stitches. *Very carefully* cut away any excess fabric.

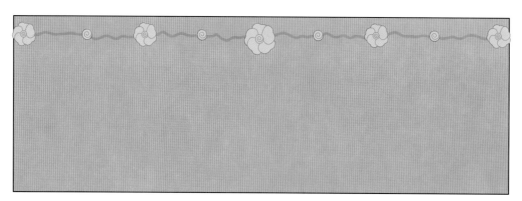

Rose and vine placement guide

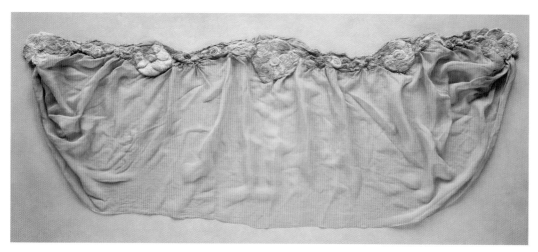

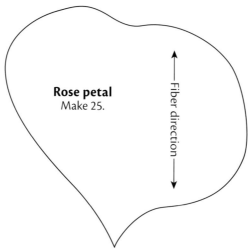

Rose petal
Make 25.

←—— Fiber direction ——→

Lost in a Meadow Bag

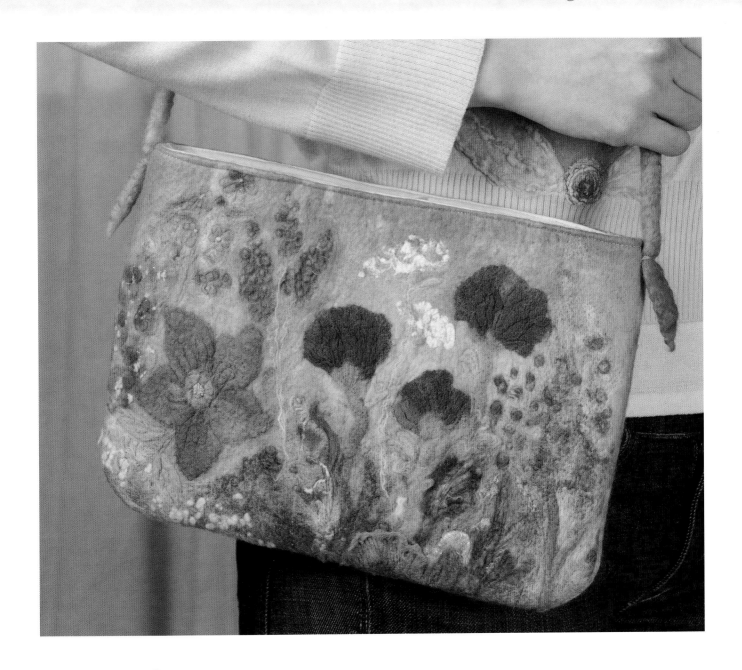

Lose yourself in a quiet leafy meadow surrounded by colorful fiber and fabric blossoms. This machine-needle-felted and wet-felted bag is sure to capture your imagination as you practice your felting techniques.

Finished size: approximately 8½" x 12", excluding strap

Materials

Bag

2 pieces, 11" x 16", of white wool prefelt fabric

2 ounces of BFL and merino mixed wool roving in variegated blues and greens

½ ounce of mixed fibers (variety of curls, fibers, yarns, and fluffed silk rods) in greens, pinks, and purples for small flowers, leaves, and stems

Small amount of yellow or gold wool roving for flowers and flower centers*

Tiny amounts of white wool nubs and white Tencel nubs

Scraps of lightweight silky fabric in bright red and/or pink for large flowers

Small amount (about a 6" piece) of deep pink roving for five-petaled flower

2 pieces, 9" x 12½", of medium-weight fusible interfacing

Clear polyester monofilament thread

Hand-needle-felting tool

2"-thick foam block

Bubble wrap or piece of solar pool cover or nylon curtain

½ yard of nylon netting

Pool noodle

Old panty hose (optional)

Small amount of dishwashing liquid

For flower centers you can also use yellow or gold yarn or ribbon.

Lining, Pocket, and Strap

2 pieces, 9" x 12½", of decorator fabric in color to coordinate with bag

9" x 9" piece of decorator fabric for pocket

Coordinating sewing thread

2 squares, 2" x 2", of fusible fleece interfacing

Magnetic snap

1 ounce of wool roving (about 42" long) in same color and fiber mix to match bag for strap

Bamboo mat

Meadow mix

 Felting Snippet

As a rule, roving is *never* cut; however, for this project I purposely cut the variegated colorways to create a "painterly" look, which is quite effective!

Instructions

1. Straighten the variegated roving and separate the colors for the field and sky by cutting between the greens and blues; the lengths should be at least 7" to 8" long. This helps create the painterly effect for our meadow. Don't worry if some colors overlap; this makes for a wonderful blending of color.

Roving cut into blue and green sections

2. Lay one piece of prefelt on top of the foam block. Split the roving down the center and very gently spread apart. Pull pieces of roving from top to bottom, creating small wisps. Starting at the top of the prefelt, begin laying out the wisps. Place very light wisps of blue fiber horizontally across the top, overlapping the wisps. Place another row beneath the first row, continuing to overlap the wisps of fiber, using more blue at the top, bluish green in the center, and green at the bottom until the entire piece is covered.

Wool layout

3. For the next layer, again start with blue at the top. However, this time, place these very light wisps of wool *vertically*. Be sure to pull the roving from top to bottom to avoid too many cut edges. When you lay out the green portion, if you slightly stagger the last row in a zigzag pattern, it will begin to have the desired painterly effect.

4. Use the hand-needle-felting tool to tack the background in place; this will make it much easier to work at your machine without wool pieces falling off. Place a piece of nylon netting temporarily over your background to keep the fibers from tangling in your needles. Beginning at the center and working outward, completely machine needle felt the entire background. Remove the netting and needle felt any spots that were missed. Be sure to keep the fabric moving under the needles.

5. Repeat steps 2–4 for the other side of the bag.

6. Place one piece of your machine-felted background on the foam block again. Working from the bottom up and following the flower placement guide on page 42, begin by placing green yarn for stems and other "leafy" greens over the background and tacking with the hand-needle-felting tool to secure. Machine needle felt in place.

7. To make the fantasy flowers, use the patterns on pages 44 and 45 to cut flowers from the silk fabric. With the machine-felted background (from step 6) on the foam block, pinch the base and, with the hand-needle-felting tool, tack in place on the background as shown below. Taking care to begin at the base, carefully manipulate the flower tops while selectively machine needle felting each in place, leaving the top slightly loose. This portion will felt down during the wet-felting process. For the base of each flower, wet a small piece of green roving in soapy water, blot on a towel, and pinch into shape, using the pattern as a guide. Machine needle felt in place to cover the bottom of each flower. This same technique can be used for the leaves. Save the leftover scraps of silk fabric.

Fantasy flowers with stems

8. For the five-petaled flower, cut a piece of pink roving about 2" to 2½" long for each petal; separate into pieces. Using the petal pattern on page 45, make a practice petal first to get a feel

for the thickness. If it's too thin, the background wool will migrate through to the top during the wet felting process. If it's too thick, the flower will look too bulky. Medium thickness works best. Briefly dip each petal in soapy water, pinch each end, and flatten out the middle to create an effective petal. With the machine-felted background (from step 7) on the foam block, place the five petals on the background as shown in the placement guide to create your flower. Tack with the hand-needle-felting tool to secure, and then machine needle felt. Dip a small piece of yellow or gold roving in soapy water and gently roll between your palms; needle felt in place in the center of the flower. (Optional: Instead of roving, make a pinwheel rose of yarn or ribbon as instructed on page 13, "Tulip Pockets," step 11.)

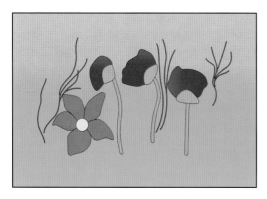

Flower placement guide

9. Needle felt curls, fibers, yarns, and/or fluffed silk rods at the bottom of your meadow, in between the flowers, to add interest and to cover the bottoms of the stems. On one side, group some wool nubs at the bottom. Cover them with netting to hold in place while machine needle felting or the needles will pierce them and pull them up. Add some Tencel nubs (these are much finer and more delicate than wool) at the top to mimic Queen Anne's lace, adding fine stems and leaves of yarn or fine strips of roving rolled between your wet palms before needling in place. Make these a little larger than you want the result to be, because they tend to shrivel a bit when needle felted.

10. Scatter flowers around the background by snipping small bits of yarns and grouping them together. Think of common flower shapes and create this illusion. (Hint: some "art" yarns are comprised of various colors, and cutting these in slices to use as flowers sometimes reveals an interesting core.)

11. Using monofilament thread in your sewing machine and beginning with the large flowers, free-motion stitch around the bottom and side edges and halfway up the petals. Stitch around the edges of each roving flower and around the center and partway out down each petal. Stitch around the background elements to create grasses and leaves and stitch small circles around the yarn snippets to create flower shapes. Remember to create your Queen Anne's lace by stitching around the Tencel nubs as well as around the wool nubs ground cover that's scattered at the bottom.

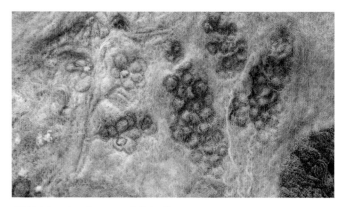

Stitching background detail

12. Place both needle-felted pieces side by side on a piece of bubble wrap and cover with a piece of netting, wet with soapy water, and rub gently for a couple of minutes. Place a pool noodle on one end of the bubble wrap and roll everything up, secure the ends with cut-off panty hose legs, and tie in a bow (this will make untying them easier); begin rolling. Roll about 100 times, unroll, and remove the netting. Rotate the pieces and roll again. Continue until it passes the pinch test. Refer to "Understanding Wet Felting and Fulling" on page 6 for more details as needed.

13. Carefully rinse in warm, soapy water, squeeze out any excess, and, one at a time, throw the pieces in the sink about 50 times. Check the pieces; if needed, throw them each a few more times until they shrink and harden. Thoroughly rinse the pieces. If desired, they can be placed in a clothes dryer on air dry for about 15 minutes to further full. Lay flat to dry. Use a pressing cloth and steam iron set on the wool setting to steam the pieces from the wrong side.

🌱 Felting Snippet 🌱

You want the result to be a nice hard felt for a bag that is durable. The back of the piece will have a nice "pebbly" appearance and the bag will not pill.

14. Fuse a piece of 9" x 12½" interfacing to the wrong side of each felted meadow piece. Using the pattern on page 46, cut out the bag front and back. Save the felt scraps. Then use the pattern to cut lining from the two pieces of 9" x 12½" decorator fabric.

15. On the right side of each lining piece, machine needle felt a vine of green yarn about ¾" from the top edge. Cut tiny leaves from the scraps and add leaf pairs along the vine here and there. Machine needle felt tiny silk scraps left over from the large flowers in between the leaves. Using monofilament thread in your sewing machine, free-motion stitch the vine, flowers,

and leaves to secure. (Optional: Embellish the pocket fabric as well.)

Bag lining fabric and embellishments

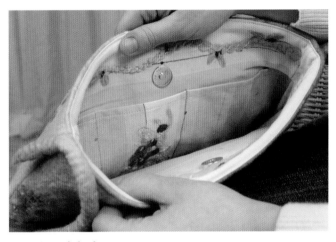

Interior of the bag

16. Fold the 9" square for the pocket in half, right sides together. Using a ¼" seam allowance, stitch around the raw edges as shown, leaving an opening to turn. Turn and press.

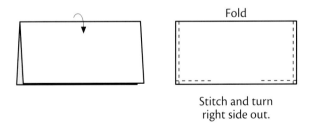

Fold

Stitch and turn
right side out.

17. On the right side of one lining piece, measure 2 ¾" down for the top. Place the pocket fold at this point and center the pocket on the lining. Stitch in place close to the edge; then stitch a line 3½" from the side to divide the pocket in two

as shown. This makes an easy-access pocket for your cell phone.

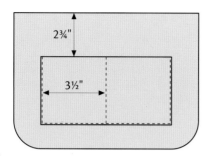

18. On the back of each lining piece, mark the center, 1½" from the top. Center a 2" square of fusible fleece interfacing over each mark and fuse in place. Mark the position of the snap washer on the fleece side; cut slits using your seam ripper, put the snap prongs through the lining, and then through the washer (on the fleece side), and bend the prongs in place. Prying them down on the edge of a worktable works well.

19. With right sides together and using a ¼" seam allowance, stitch the bag front and back together, beginning at one side and continuing around the bottom and up the other side. Turn the bag right side out.

20. With right sides together and using a ¼" seam allowance, stitch the lining together, leaving a 5" opening in the bottom to pull the bag through.

21. Place the bag inside the lining with right sides together, matching the raw edges. Using a ¼" seam allowance, stitch around the top of the lining and bag. Turn your bag to the right side through the lining; press using a press cloth and stitch the opening in the lining closed. Topstitch around the bag top.

22. To make a cord for the strap, you'll need a 42"-long piece of roving split down the center for a finished 36"-long strap. Wet the length of roving in soapy water and place on a towel. Begin gently rolling one section at a time between your palms until the cord starts to form; then use more and more strength to form the roll, tapering the ends in a point. Briefly dip the hardened cord into soapy water and blot on a towel. Place the cord a section at a time on a bamboo mat, fold the mat over the cord, and roll back and forth until the cord hardens some more. Continue doing this until the cord is quite hard (it may seem really hard while it's wet but will get softer as it dries). Rewet and rework some more. Rinse well and leave until dry. Attach the cord to the sides of your bag by securely hand sewing through the side seams.

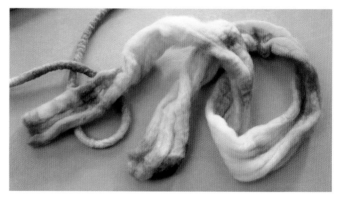

Wool roving for bag strap

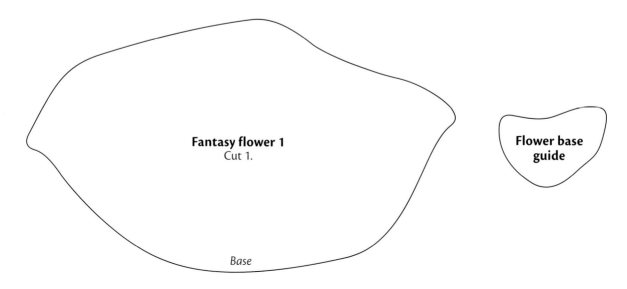

Fantasy flower 1
Cut 1.

Base

Flower base guide

Detail from opposite side of the bag

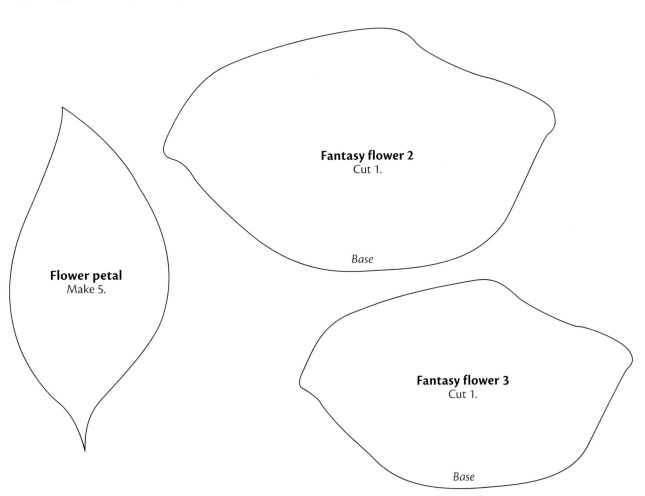

Flower petal
Make 5.

Fantasy flower 2
Cut 1.

Base

Fantasy flower 3
Cut 1.

Base

Bag
Cut 2 for bag
and 2 for lining.

Place on fold.

¼" seam allowance

Resources

Prefelts, Roving, and Supplies for Wet Felting

Outback Fibers
Georgetown, Texas
www.outbackfibers.com
800-276-5015

New England Felting Supply
Easthampton, Massachusetts
www.feltingsupply.com
413-527-1188

Ewe Give Me the Knits
Victoria, Australia
www.ewegivemetheknits.com

Frabjous Fibers
South Newfane, Vermont
www.frabjousfibers.com
802-257-4178
Sea Mist Merino and BFL for Lost in a Meadow Bag

Studio-Loo
Toronto, Ontario, Canada
www.studioloo.com
Rose fiber for Leafy Rose Wrap

Spritely Goods
Phoenix, Arizona
www.spritelygoods.com

Holly EQQ
Gulf Coast, Florida
www.hollyeqq.com
Woodrose fiber for Leafy Rose Wrap

Dollmakers Ink
Chesapeake, Virginia
www.dollmakersink.com
757-436-1316
Mulberry paper for Tea Party Cozy

Joggles
West Warwick, Rhode Island
www.joggles.com
401-615-7696
Nubs—wool and Tencel for Queen Anne's lace in Lost in a Meadow Bag

Paradise Fibers
Spokane, Washington
www.paradisefibers.net
888-320-7746

Forestheart Studio
Woodsboro, Maryland
www.forestheart.com
301-845-4447

Silk Fibers

The Yarn Tree
Brooklyn, New York
www.theyarntree.com
718-384-8030

Treenway Silks
Salt Spring Island, British Columbia, Canada
www.treenwaysilks.com
888-383-7455
Silk hankies for Flower Fairy Lampshade

Confections, Wool Curls, Fiber Packs, and Fancy Batts

Her Majesty Margo
Mount Airy, Maryland
www.hermajestymargo.com
301-831-3773
Custom orders upon request

Wool and Silk Fabrics, Wool Roving, and Yarns

Dharma Trading Company
San Rafael, California
www.dharmatrading.com
800-542-5227

Vogue Fabrics
Evanston, Illinois
www.voguefabricsstore.com
800-433-4313

Vilene Water-Soluble Fabric

All Stitch LLC
Baltimore, Maryland
www.allstitch.net
410-646-0382

Pointe to Pointe (59" wide)
Lecanto, Florida
www.pointetopointe.com
888-266-8933

Rowenta Steam Generator

Joann.com
www.joann.com
888-739-4120

Colorhue Dye

Silk Things
www.silkthings.com
425-821-2287

Hand-Dyed Silk Ribbon

Artemis
www.artemisinc.com
888-233-5187
Hanah ribbon for Tulip Pockets

About the Author

Margo Duke of Her Majesty Margo wearing her "Tigress" machine-needle-felted scarf

Margo Duke enjoyed learning how to knit and crochet from each of her grandmothers at an early age while growing up in Scotland, and she's constantly been doing some sort of handwork ever since. Margo loves working with color, fabric, and fiber and enjoys a wide variety of needlework. In fact, her mother's family comes from Stornoway (a magical isle in the North of Scotland), and some family members were weavers of Harris tweed; they still live in the same croft today where they worked on their loom. The croft is surrounded by flocks of sheep roaming the wild terrain. Working with fiber awakened a creativity that was dormant in Margo's genes; she will never forget her trip there. And what a very special memory it is: on her visit she sat in a small church on a hill listening to the congregation singing the Psalms while overlooking the peaceful site of a cemetery sloping down to the water.

Margo taught herself English smocking and heirloom embroidery in the early 1970s before it became popular. She loved the process of pleating and stitching fine fabrics, combining them with lace, and adding just the right fine detail. She created commissioned Christening gowns and taught her craft for many years. Margo also loves piecing quilts—especially for special gifts. However, these days most of her time is spent with her felting and fiber obsession—thinking, designing, experimenting, creating, teaching, and everything else that goes along with it, such as the hunt for that perfect curl or color. She believes that spending daily time with one's Bliss is an absolute essential to a healthy and well-balanced life (and who are we kidding—it's fun too!).

Margo is fortunate to have a loving and supportive husband and family and hopes to pass along some of her fiber skills to her five grandchildren—and anyone else who will listen!